S T E M DETECTIVES

THE CASE OF THE MISSING NOODLES

WRITTEN BY
William Anthony

DESIGNED BY
Danielle Webster-Jones

ookLife
UBLISHING

2020

ookLife Publishing Ltd.
ng's Lynn
orfolk, PE30 4LS

BN: 978-1-78637-986-3

A catalogue record for this book is available from the British Library.

All rights reserved. Printed in Malaysia.

Photo Credits: All images courtesy of Shutterstock. With thanks to Getty Images, Thinkstock Photo and iStockphoto. Cover & throughout– Jemastock, Macrovector, ProStockStudio, stickerama, MicroOne, tn-prints – Gaidamashchuk, Golden Vector, MaryDesy, Monash. 2 – Tartila. 6 – Magura, What's My Name, ProStockStudio. 10 – Ilya Bolotov. 18 – Pechonkin Denys. 19 – MSSA. 23 – WICHIAN SAELEE.
Additional illustration by Amy Li & Danielle Webster-Jones.

Written by:
William Anthony

Edited by:
Robin Twiddy

Designed by:
Danielle Webster-Jones

EVIDENCE BOARD

Welcome, new recruit! We're out solving a case right now, but we'll be back soon. We're so happy that you want to join the (STEM Detectives.) We're experts in STEM, which stands for science, technology, engineering and maths. But for us, STEM stands for something else too...

We are the Special Team for Ending Mayhem!

THE TEAM

KIM
Science Boss

SANJAY
Tech Whizz

LUCAS
Engineering Ace

ASHA
Maths Queen

iGUMBO
RoboDog Sidekick

THE BRIEF

Trouble is never far away for the STEM Detectives, and they need your help to solve this case. When you see this symbol, they will ask you to figure out a problem, do an experiment or look for clues. Complete each task before you turn the page.
You can check your answers on page 24.

Today was supposed to be the best day of the year. It was **Noodle Day** at Stemberry School, and the yearly show was taking place that afternoon.

When everyone arrived, all the lights were off and the noodles had been stolen. This was the last thing the STEM Detectives needed this early in the morning.

Kitchen closed - noodles gone.

The Three Little Wigs

They each had starring roles in the yearly show — The Three Little Wigs — and they only had a few hours before showtime. "We've solved crimes this quickly before and we can do it again," said Asha.

"We'd better get started, then," said Sanjay. "First, we need to get these lights back on," added Kim. "Caretaker Bob can help us do that." Time was ticking away for the Detectives...

Bob was using the darkness as an excuse to nap. "BOB!" shouted Lucas. "Someone has cut out the lights and used the darkness to steal the Noodle Day noodles!" Bob was a little flustered.

"Err... right... let's check the circuit for a break," he said.

Look at this map of the school. The lights circuit is shown by all the dots connected with **BLUE** lines. If a part of the circuit is broken, two of the dots that should be connected are not. Can you find the room with the broken circuit?

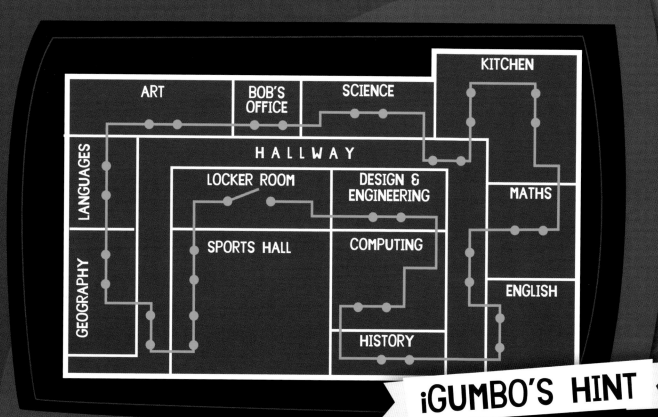

WE NEED YOU!

You think it's broken in the locker room? I think you're right.

"It's the locker room. Quick, we don't have much time left! Bob, bring your tools!" ordered Lucas. When the STEM Detectives arrived in the locker room, there was a broken cable on the floor. Bob got to work.

Kim spotted an open locker. Was this the noodle thief's locker? Inside, there was a magnet and three keys. "Over here, STEM Detectives," she called. "I think our thief used a magnet to steal the key to the kitchen."

The noodle thief might have used a magnet to steal the kitchen key, but there are three keys here. One is plastic, one is rubber and one is metal. We can do an experiment to find out which key is the right one!

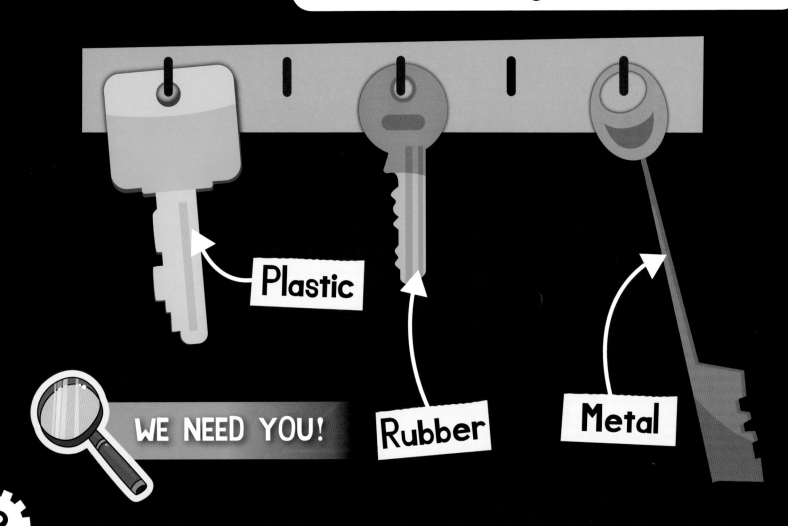

Plastic

Rubber

Metal

WE NEED YOU!

Tallies are used to keep track of things. Each line equals one thing. Tallies are drawn in groups of five. The fifth line is drawn across the middle of the other four lines. Can you work out how many things have been found and how many have been lost?

LOST:
卌 卌 ||

FOUND:
卌 卌 卌 卌 |||

WE NEED YOU!

iGUMBO'S HINT

卌 = 5 | = 1

18 found and 12 lost? I wonder what the tallies are for...

"Got it!" shouted Bob from the darkness. One by one, the lights flickered back on. "We've got about 10 minutes before the show; we need to be quick. Let's go to the crime scene and see what we can find," said Lucas.

When the STEM Detectives reached the kitchen, there was no lock for the stolen key. If the key wasn't for the kitchen, what was it for?

"I have an idea!" yelled Sanjay. "We can use the kitchen computer to see if there are any clues in the food log!"

The computer wouldn't turn on. Time was running out. Sanjay looked at the back. There was a gap with nothing plugged in and five wires lying on the floor.

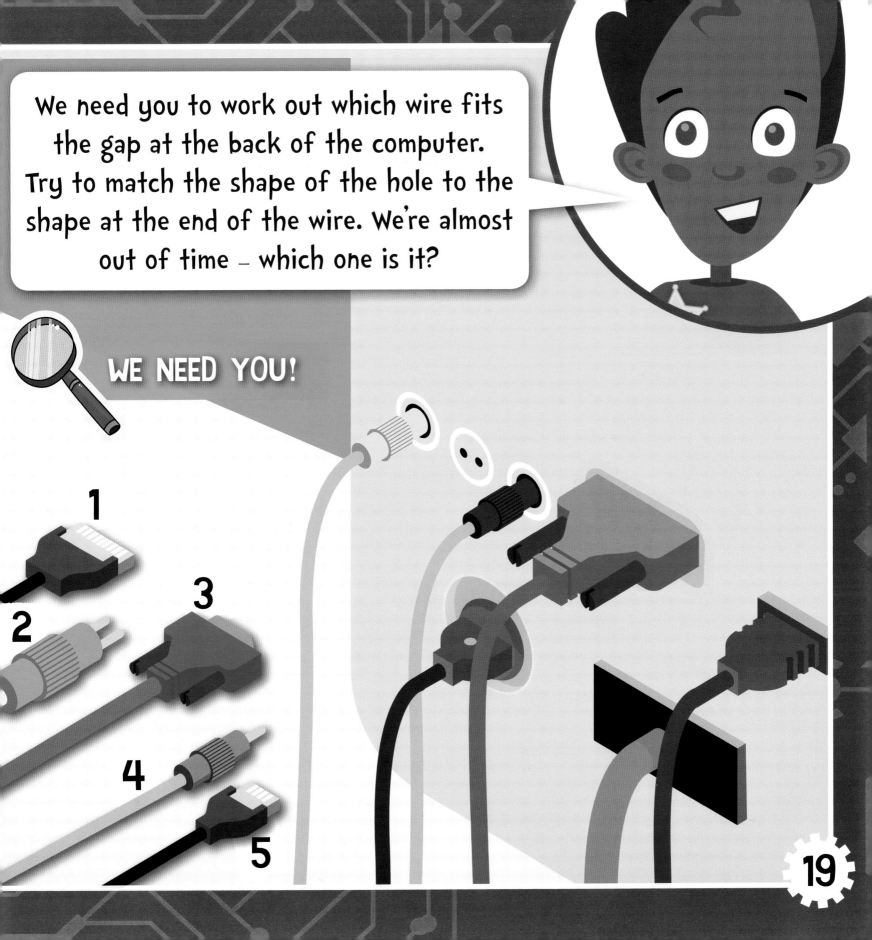

Number 2? Let's plug it in!

"It's turning on!" cheered Kim, but it was too late. It was showtime. The STEM Detectives felt odd; they'd never left a case unsolved before. The detectives had to move on — after all, the show, and the wigs, must go on!

The STEM Detectives sat in front of their drama teacher, Mr P Former. "I've got some bad news," he said. "I lost **12** of the wigs for the show." Asha's eyes grew wider. The tally from the noodle thief's locker said **12** things were missing...

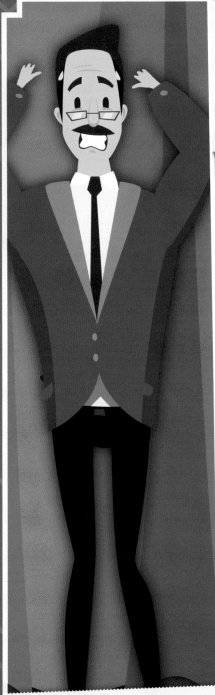

"I've had a terrible day," started Mr P Former.

"I had to make a tally of all the wigs I'd lost..."

LOST:
𝍸𝍸 𝍸𝍸 ||

FOUND:
𝍸𝍸 𝍸𝍸 𝍸𝍸 |||

"... and then I tripped over a wire and broke it..."

"... before dropping my costume-cupboard key in the dark. Luckily, I had a magnet to help me find it."

Everything started to make sense to the STEM Detectives. "You stole the noodles!" yelled Lucas.

"Borrowed," corrected Mr P Former. "I was going to put them back! But for now, I've fixed the problem of the lost wigs..."

WELL DONE!

You helped us solve the case! We couldn't have done it without your super skills in science, technology, engineering and maths. You've earned the right to wear a STEM Detectives badge!

Scan this QR code, print off your badge and fix it to your top. We'll see you on our next adventure!

SOLUTIONS

PAGE 9

OFFICE	
HALLWAY	
LOCKER ROOM	D ENG
SPORTS HALL	CO

PAGE 13

If the experiment worked, the metal paperclip will have been the only object attracted to the magnet. This means that the metal key is the correct one.

PAGE 15

Found: |||| |||| |||| |||
5 + 5 + 5 + 3 = 18

Lost: |||| |||| ||
5 + 5 + 2 = 12

PAGE 19

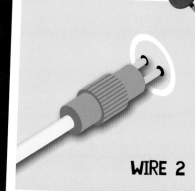

WIRE 2